to my dear friend:

_____

from:

_____

Friendship Promises

Friendship Promises

Two are better than one.

ECCLESIASTES 4:9

B&H
PUBLISHING GROUP

NASHVILLE, TENNESSEE

In our friendship, I promise to be:

This is my friendship promise to you.

The Gift OF Authenticity

4

Let's be authentic
in our friendship,
sharing the beauty
of our too-loud laughter
and awkward tears.

I WILL BE "UN-FINE" WITH YOU

Nothing is riskier or more vulnerable than cracking open the doors of my messy home, let alone the doors of my actual life. I get so used to neatly packaged people and stories and families that I can forget how to be anything but "fine" when someone asks. Because, deep down, there are messes much messier than the dust bunnies or gritty dishes. There are fears and doubts and despair and broken places that cut so deep it takes the breath away.

I nod and smile and say I'm fine, the kids are fine, work is fine, marriage is fine, just fine, thanks for asking. And all the while there's this big, messy, gaping wound bleeding raw right through my perfectly fine outfit that I hope no one notices. All the while I'm desperate for somebody to care enough to see.

Fine is so dangerous, isn't it? Fine means the end of a conversation; the beginning of nothing. Now it's time for the battle cry that if Truth can set us free (John 8:32), it's best to start living in those places. Maybe going first and admitting my un-fine isn't a weakness; instead, I will see it as a gift to you, who can finally exhale and admit your un-fine too. This is my friendship promise to you.

Let's do it; let's be un-fine together, eh?

Love
one another
DEEPLY
as brothers and sisters.
OUTDO one another in
showing honor.

ROMANS 12:10

I will dare to be "un-fine"
in our friendship, letting you
into my messy spaces and
entering into yours.

CONSIDER THE BLESSING OF FRIENDS WHO
ARE AUTHENTIC, EVEN WHEN THAT AUTHENTICITY
MEANS AN INVITATION INTO THEIR MESSY PLACES.

LORD, OPEN MY HEART *to*

the women right in front of me.
Help me show my friends that they are
precious, beautiful gifts to me. I want to
demonstrate through my friendship that
You created them exactly the way they
are for a unique purpose.

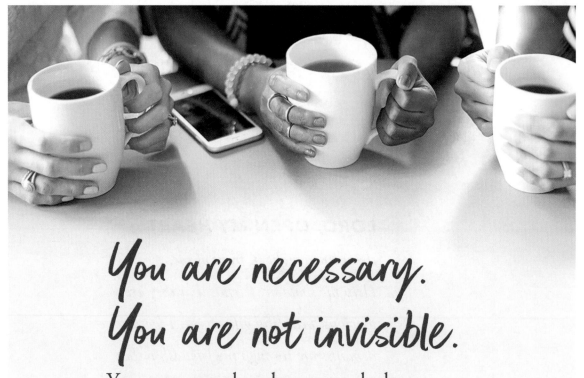

You are necessary.
You are not invisible.

You are named and seen, and please
don't erase your relevance because
you think you're not relevant to the
people you pass by on a screen.

GOD is LOVE,
and the one who
REMAINS in LOVE
remains in God,
AND
God REMAINS in him.

1 JOHN 4:16

Let's commit to sharing our stories first so that our friends can feel comfortable opening up about theirs.

THINK OF A TIME WHEN GOD USED YOUR
CLOSEST FRIENDS TO REVEAL HIMSELF AND
SPEAK TRUTH INTO YOUR LIFE.

LORD, YOU CREATED ME *to connect and be in relationship, with You and with others. May I embrace the unique purpose You've given both myself and my friends, celebrating our differences and like- nesses. For we're all made in Your wondrous and glorious image. And You are good and holy and true.*

IN HIS IMAGE

In the beginning God made us in His image. It's the only image we're supposed to fit. The only image that won't make us feel like we can't breathe because everything is too tight or too uncomfortable or too itchy and scratchy in all the wrong places.

I promise to you that I won't cram myself—like the feet of Cinderella's sisters— into shoes I was never meant to wear. Those shoes, like the ridiculous images that were designed with us in mind, are something I never want to force myself or you as my friend into.

I promise to be my authentic, God-created self with you, and I promise to accept you for the unique and beautiful creation you are as well as the Christlike image God is molding you into.

One with
MANY FRIENDS
may be harmed
BUT
THERE is a FRIEND
who stays CLOSER
than a BROTHER.

PROVERBS 18:24

This is your one beautiful life. God has invited you into it to live as you, not anyone else.

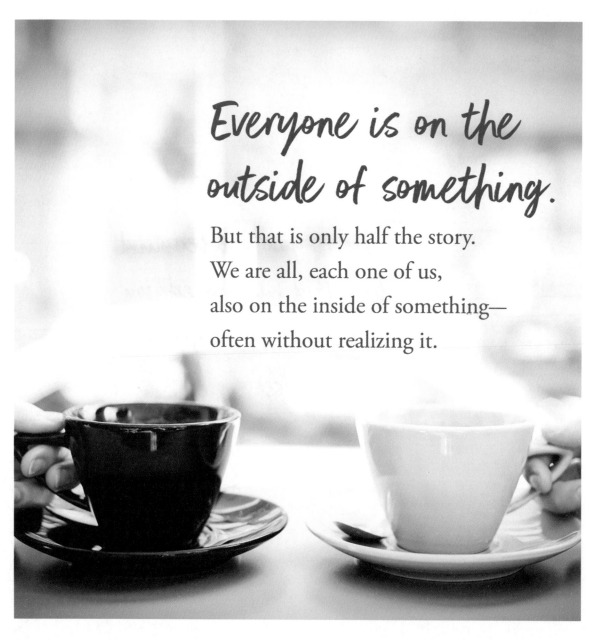

Everyone is on the outside of something.

But that is only half the story.
We are all, each one of us,
also on the inside of something—
often without realizing it.

FATHER, I PRAY *that we may be open to be seen. Really seen. And in that openness, that we may find our people and real friendships because You desire for us to walk together.*

You are the LIGHT of the WORLD ...let your light SHINE before others, so that they may SEE your GOOD WORKS and GIVE GLORY to your FATHER in heaven.

MATTHEW 5:14-16

HOW CAN I BE A LIGHT IN MY FRIENDSHIPS,
SHOWING OTHERS MY AUTHENTIC SELF AND
ENCOURAGING THEM TO DO THE SAME?

Bearing with one another and forgiving one another if anyone has a grievance against another. Just as the Lord has FORGIVEN you so you are also to FORGIVE.

COLOSSIANS 3:13

The Gift
OF Being Present

Friendship was
breathed into our DNA
at the very beginning.

I INVITE YOU IN

When I read about the early church in the book of Acts, I am blessed, encouraged, and challenged. They did life together in every way possible. They worshiped together, broke bread together, and studied the Scriptures together. And they continued to pursue community with one another. When you and I embrace a James 1:19 way of living in community, it can speak volumes to the world around us and gives us the opportunity to invite others to join us to live a life where sisters in Christ genuinely love, care for, and honor each other.

It's been said that God gave us two ears and one mouth so that we can listen twice as much as we speak. I want to learn to listen with my ears, heart, and mind open to you and the Lord. I promise to always believe the best in you, offer you the benefit of the doubt when friendship is hard work, and extend grace as often as possible.

It's not always easy or natural to view others through the lens of Christ. But this is what it really means to be present in our friendships. After all, when God is quick to hear, slow to speak, and slow to anger, how can I respond with anything less?

Everyone should be
QUICK to LISTEN,
SLOW to SPEAK,
AND
SLOW to ANGER.

JAMES 1:19

In our friendship,
let's vow to be quick
to listen, slow to speak,
and slow to become angry
with each other.

REFLECT ON THE BLESSING OF FRIENDS
WHO ARE QUICKER TO LISTEN THAN TO
SPEAK, WHO OPERATE IN GRACE INSTEAD
OF IN ANGER.

GOD, THANK YOU *for being so quick to listen to Your people and for being slow to anger. Help me to follow Your example in my relationships, offering patience and encouragement to the women I'm blessed to call friends. Let them know that they are heard, cared for, and invited—both into my life and into Your family.*

Maybe the most **_intimate, radical thing_** we can do for our friends is show up.

Again, truly I tell you,
IF TWO OF YOU on earth
agree about a matter
that you PRAY for,
it WILL be DONE
for you by my
FATHER in HEAVEN.

MATTHEW 18:19

I commit to being present
in our friendship,
even when that simply
means showing up.

WHAT IS AN EASY WAY TO INCORPORATE
THE BEAUTY OF PRAYER AND PRESENCE
INTO FRIENDSHIPS?

I'm sure I won't always get it right, but I'll keep showing up. With encouragement instead of competition. With Kleenex, big news or sad news, on the bad hair days and the Mondays, and all the in-between days with their ordinary news too.

OH LORD, HELP ME TO BE A LISTENER. *A welcomer. A woman who looks for authentic conversations. Please open my eyes to intentionally look for opportunities to draw others in. Let my welcoming heart be the open canvas that allows the sharing and giving in friendship to become our tangible art.*

It's counter cultural
to refuse to utter those three
words we say without even
thinking, "I'm too busy."
I don't want to be too busy.
I want to be available.

OPENING THE DOOR

If I wait for my house or my life to be perfect before inviting you into it, I might never let you come through the door.

"Hospitality is not about inviting people into our perfect home; it is all about inviting people into our imperfect hearts." – Rush Soukup

I sometimes feel vulnerable when you step over the threshold and pick your way in between the layers of chaos that say, 'We live here. And we've never got it perfect.' I still prefer the days you drop by when candles are lit and carpets are vacuumed. But if I believe what I say about friendship, then that includes the messy days. The ones where I've been too tired to catch up on much of anything.

It includes welcoming you into the nooks and crannies of my ordinary and remembering not to be ashamed. Remembering that to become real, friendship more often than not requires becoming comfortable with the snapshots of life often taken at an unflattering angle.

So, I will open my front door to your friendship, in spite of my mess and insecurities.

Because I want you here. Whether I'm ever perfectly ready or not. I want you. Just the way you are. Which will likely mean most days, I must open the door just the way I am too.

If I wait for my house or my life to be perfect before inviting someone into it,

I might never let anyone come through the door.

Love
one another
as I have loved you.
No one has
GREATER LOVE
than this:
to LAY DOWN HIS LIFE
for his friends.

JOHN 15:12-13

Laying our lives down for our friends can translate into a hundred daily inconveniences that simply remind her without using actual words, "You are not alone."

THINK OF WAYS THAT MAKING SMALL SACRIFICES
FOR FRIENDS DEMONSTRATES "LAYING DOWN OUR
LIVES" FOR THE SAKE OF OTHERS?

I want you here. Whether I'm ever perfectly ready or not. I want you. Just the way you are. So, I will open the door just the way I am too.

FATHER GOD, I PRAISE YOU

for Your goodness, mercy, and grace. I marvel that You showed us how to love others through the life of Your Son. Remove my blinders that I might see the people right in front of me who need to be loved.

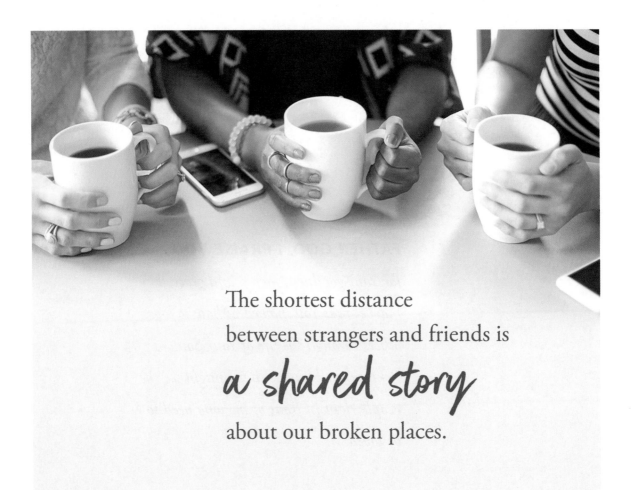

The shortest distance
between strangers and friends is

a shared story

about our broken places.

The Gift of Encouragement

Spur one another on toward love, courage, goodness, and a God who is intimately in love with us all.

ENCOURAGEMENT OVER AGENDA

ENCOURAGEMENT AND ENVY CAN'T COEXIST—our friendship is healthiest when we can look past our fears and focus on how we can encourage each other. We move from a "what's in it for me" focus and instead ask God how we can love each other in a way that honors both one another and Him.

WHEN I ENCOURAGE YOU, I SHOW THAT I LOVE YOU MORE THAN I LOVE MY OWN AGENDA. I will choose to elevate you, spurring you on towards the Father, instead of elevating my own platform and personal agenda.

Lifting you up lifts me as well—**THE BEST FRIENDS ARE THE ONES WHO SEE THE POTENTIAL IN OTHERS AND HELP THEM SHINE IN THEIR STRENGTHS.** Using my gifts to help you in strengthening yours sharpens us both.

So then,
let us pursue
what promotes
peace
and what
builds up
one
another.

ROMANS 14:19

The best friends are the ones who see the potential in others and help them shine in their strengths.

HOW HAS ENCOURAGEMENT FROM MY FRIENDS POINTED ME TO JESUS?

LORD GOD, THANK YOU *for the gift of words and the beauty of language. Help me to steward my words well, to honor you and others with my speech. May I speak out of the overflow of grace and kindness, the fruits of your indwelling Holy Spirit. Teach me to tame my tongue, and use my words to build others up.*

The secret to finding and keeping lasting friendships: become women who want to see the women around them flourish.

Carry one another's BURDENS; in this way YOU will FULFILL the law of Christ.

GALATIANS 6:2

Carrying each other's
burdens provides a safe
space for each other and
is encouraging to our souls.

WHAT ARE SOME SIMPLE WAYS TO ENCOURAGE MY FRIENDS THROUGH LOVE, KINDNESS, AND GRACE?

LORD, IT'S SO EASY TO FEEL LIKE I SHOULD BE STRONG WHEN I'M NOT. *The truth is, I'm weak but I don't like to show it. It's hard to be real with other people, and sometimes it's hard for me to be real with You because I think You expect me to have more faith and courage. Help me to remember that in my weakness, I can depend on You and Your strength. I know that's where Your power shows up and Your glory shows off when people see my need for You.*

The words we say to ourselves matter because the God who is **The Word says we matter.** And it's time we start believing Him.

Share this truth with a friend who needs encouragement!

SHARPENING KINDLY

Though sharpening the way God intended may sting as rough edges come off, the process is always meant to be kind. A friendship where both people enter genuine and true, shedding their layers at the door, opening up with one another as who they are—instead of who they think they should be—is absolute authenticity.

You see, God meets us both exactly where we are. He simply asks us to be authentic and real with our Lord—to rip off the masks the world suggests we keep and instead rest in who He created us to be.

God designed these sharpening kinds of friendships so they run deep, and wide, and deeper still. The shallow waters are not where we become sharpened. Safety is not where we grow. Only when we take risks—when we're vulnerable, authentic, and held accountable—can we realize how much more freeing it is in the deep. Only when we dive can we understand what we'd be missing if we stayed on the shore.

I commit to taking risks and diving into the deep waters of friendship so that we both may be sharpened.

I commit to taking risks and diving into the deep waters of friendship so that we both may be strengthened.

FATHER, HELP ME TO DIVE IN THE DEEP WATERS—*both with You and my dear friends. Rid me of the fear of vulnerability that keeps me in the shallow water, and instead help me to sharpen them with a heart full of the kindness and love You've shown me.*

Jonathan was bound to David in close friendship, and LOVED him as much as he loved himself.

1 SAMUEL 18:1

HOW CAN I BLESS A FRIEND WITH ENCOURAGEMENT SO SHE KNOWS HOW MUCH I CARE?

Loyalty in friendship
is an extension of the
covenant kindness shown
to us by the Lord.

HEAVENLY FATHER, THANK YOU FOR LOVING ME. *Thank You for LOVING ME! I am blown away by this amazing love. Help me put on love-colored glasses so I can see how especially fond of others You are. I want to live and act in a way that reminds others of that love. I want to walk in step with You and love my neighbors in a way that shows them You.*

Some of the best and hardest
work God calls us to do is

love other people.

The Gift
OF Being Rooted

True community cannot
exist unless it is rooted
in the Father.

EMBRACING COMMUNITY

Some days we are running on empty, desperate for encouragement or appreciation or for someone to simply see us. And it's wonderful when we get that encouragement from our friends.

However, if we are constantly disappointed by how our friends don't live up to our need for encouragement, the problem might be that we're expecting the kind of soul validation they're not equipped to give. Latching on to a friend with the hope that she will give us God-sized affirmation will always disappoint. This is neither our friend's fault nor our own. This is just how we're designed—to crave the acceptance and approval only God can provide.

God never tires of us needing him so desperately. Instead, He is delighted—and He never, ever withholds His validation from me. Or from you. And that kind of security? It can change a girl. It tattoos acceptance into her bones and anchors her identity in the God who is obsessed with spending time with us. And it teaches her to let go of her death grip on the opinions of others, making possible a guilt-free friendship.

Above all, put on LOVE, which is the perfect bond of unity.

COLOSSIANS 3:14

May all of my friendships be rooted in the foundation of my relationship with the Father.

HOW HAVE I SEEN GOD AT WORK IN MY LIFE THROUGH THE BLESSING OF MY FRIENDSHIPS?

LORD, I PRAY *that we would be overcome by Your presence in such a way that we can't help but share Your mighty acts with our friends and family. As we become so aware of Your presence in all of the beautiful, ordinary moments of our day, may we experience Your goodness and glory and declare without hesitation Your mighty name, Your mighty acts, and Your miraculous grace.*

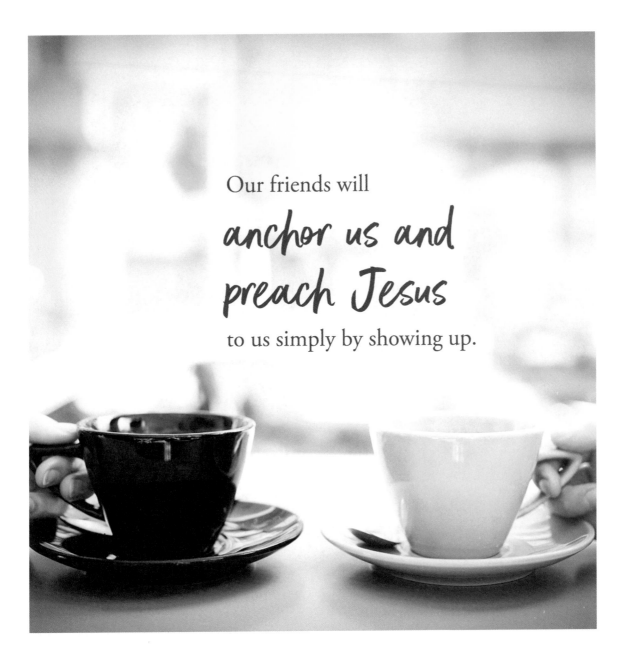

Our friends will

anchor us and preach Jesus

to us simply by showing up.

But the wisdom from above is first PURE, then PEACE-LOVING, gentle, compliant, full of MERCY and GOOD FRUITS, unwavering, without pretense.

JAMES 3:17

God, grant me
opportunities to love
my friends from the
overflow of love You've
demonstrated to me.

HOW CAN MY FRIENDSHIPS BE IMPACTED BY THE
KNOWLEDGE THAT EACH OF US IS CHOSEN BY GOD?

JESUS, IT IS IN YOU *that we live, move, and have our being. Thank You for making us come alive. Thank You for abundant life. As I eagerly anticipate the gifts of the future, please don't let me miss that beauty that surrounds me—right here, right now.*

Jesus is never tired of us always needing Him. Instead

He is delighted

by how desperately we need His validation and He never, ever witholds it from us.

THE "MORE"
OF FRIENDSHIP:

God, I have found, is stubborn. And He has stubbornly insisted that there is no "done" when it comes to sacrificial love. There is only "more." More listening. More changing. More bending. More willingness to be open. More awkward and more choosing to stay instead of cutting loose and quitting. He has walked me down the winding corridors of "more" miles and miles farther than I ever would have thought my legs or my heart could take.

He's always been intimately involved and insanely patient. With me. And it has changed me. That's the kicker. It has changed *me* when I thought it was about changing the other person. It has taken apart all my assumptions about love and kindness and patience and that old-school word *long-suffering* and put them back together again in a picture that demonstrates how eternal God's patience is with me. With all of us.

Being willing to let God work in me and through me for the sake of friendship has been nothing short of miraculous. So, I commit to allowing the Lord to work through me for the sake of strengthening our friendship and growing closer both to God and to you, dear friend.

May I receive the "more" of God's sacrificial love in order to demonstrate that love in my friendships.

GOD, GIVE ME EYES *to see who You truly are—full of sacrificial love and patience for me. I receive Your love and patience as gifts and ask that as I begin to comprehend the expanse of Your love and grace toward me, I would be able to extend those things to the friends You've blessed me with.*

My grace is sufficient for you, for my power is perfected in weakness.

2 CORINTHIANS 12:9

WHAT COULD SERVE AS A DAILY REMINDER THAT
JESUS LOVES ME INTIMATELY (AND LOVES OTHERS
AROUND ME THE SAME)?

Knowing God makes
being known by others
possible and beautiful.

LORD, SHOW US THE GATES *of friendship we've built for ourselves. Grant us Your Spirit, that we may put on love every day, and in so doing, that we may love well beyond the gate, for Your glory.*

Neither Facebook nor Instagram, mean girls nor church cliques will be able to separate us from the radical never-giving-up, never-looking-back, always-believing-the-best *love of God.*

The CSB (in)courage Devotional Bible

invites every woman to find her story *within the* greatest story ever told— God's story *of* redemption.

- **312 devotions** by 122 (in)courage community writers

- 10 distinct thematic **reading plans**

- Stories of courage from **50 women** of the Bible

- *and more features!*

Find out more at **incourageBible.com**

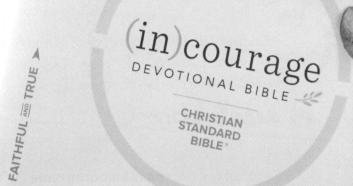

(in)courage

FIND YOURSELF AMONG FRIENDS

To say *we love community* might be an understatement.

At (in)courage, our hearts beat for strong, healthy, God-honoring friendship.

Nothing brings us more joy than watching like-hearted women *connect.*

Connecting with others lightens the load and adds space for more laughter — and healing — because we know

we aren't alone.

Join us at **www.incourage.me** & connect with us on social media!

@incourage

Come on in!

Hospitality is one of the best ways to live out the two greatest commandments: Loving *God* with all your heart and loving your *neighbor* as yourself.

Resources to help you change the world around you, one open door at a time.

Book
justopenthedoor.com

Bible Study
lifeway.com/justopenthedoor

A Study of Biblical Hospitality

VIDEO-BASED
7-SESSION BIBLE STUDY

Just Open the Door

BIBLE STUDY

(in)courage author
JEN SCHMIDT

Just Open the Door

How **One** Invitation **Can** Change a Generation